TONY EVANS

Speaks Out On

A WOMAN'S ROLE IN THE HOME

TONY EVANS

Speaks Out On

A WOMAN'S ROLE IN THE HOME

MOODY PUBLISHERS

CHICAGO

We hope you enjoy this book from Moody Publishers. Our goal is to provide high-quality, thought-provoking books and products that connect truth to your real needs and challenges. For more information on other books and products written and produced from a biblical perspective, go to www.moodypublishers.com or write to:

Moody Publishers
820 N. LaSalle Boulevard
Chicago, IL 60610

ISBN-10: 0-8024-4377-X
ISBN-13: 978-0-8024-4377-9

7 9 10 8

Printed in the United States of America

A WOMAN'S ROLE IN THE HOME

The story is told of two escaped prisoners who were on the run through the woods when they heard the tracking dogs barking behind them and realized the guards were closing in. The first prisoner scrambled up a tree in the hopes of throwing the dogs off, so the second prisoner decided he would do the same thing and ran to a nearby tree, which he also climbed.

As the prisoners hid among the branches and listened, the dogs grew closer. Before long they were barking at the base of the tree where the first prisoner was hiding. He was a quick thinker, so he started saying, "Coo, coo, coo."

The prison guards jerked the dogs back from the tree and said, "Come on, let's go. There's nothing up there but a bird."

Then the guards came to the tree where the second prisoner was hiding. As the dogs started barking and jumping at the tree, this prisoner panicked. He wasn't as quick as the first prisoner, but he had heard the guy throw the dogs off by making a bird noise and realized he also needed to make some kind of animal sound. So he thought for a minute and then said, "Moo, moo, moo."

When you're confused about what you are supposed to be doing, you wind up making the wrong noise at the wrong time in the wrong place! We see Christian couples today who are making a lot of noise, complaining about their spouses and their marriages, when the truth is they have neglected their own biblical roles and become confused about what they are supposed to be doing. We could say they're mooing when they ought to be cooing.

Now I want you to know right up front that even though this booklet focuses on the woman's role in the home, nothing we have to say here is meant to excuse men who aren't performing their God-given role as husbands. In fact, when I presented this material on marriage to the congregation at our church in Dallas, I began by addressing the husbands as those command-ed to lead, not the wives.

Since you don't have that material in front of you, let me summarize it by saying that the primary respon-sibility for the health of a marriage falls on the hus-band, not the wife. It's true that there are wives who are not fulfilling their biblical role, but that doesn't change the fact that husbands are charged with pri-mary responsibility to see that their marriages function as God intended. And the best way they can do this is by taking seriously their role as lovers and spiritual leaders.

I say this so you won't think that wives are being singled out to bear the primary load of responsibility to make their marriages function as God intended. Many women say they *want* their husbands to step up to the plate and assume leadership in the home, relieving them of a burden they know they are not designed to carry and would gladly yield if their husbands would come through for them.

Since we deal with the husband's responsibilities in detail in another place, I want to focus on the wife's role here. Actually, both spouses' roles are summarized in Ephesians 5:33: "Each individual among you also is to love his own wife even as himself, and the wife must see to it that she respects her husband."

A husband is commanded to love his wife, even if he may not like her at the moment, and a wife is commanded to respect her husband even if she isn't feeling kind toward him at the moment. But too many Christian women are taking their marriage cues from television or their girlfriends instead of from God's Word.

Many women who are now wives were raised in single-parent homes and in a matriarchal environment over which they had no control. The problem is that they have come to think this is how things are supposed to be. Since mama ran their home, they figure they need to run their home now that they're married.

But a woman who tries to take charge of her marriage

is trampling on the respect that she owes to her husband and that God commands her to give to her husband. Many men are functioning as poor husbands at least in part because their wives are operating far outside of God's standard.

So in this booklet we want to find out what a wife's biblical role entails and what a woman looks and acts like when she is fulfilling her calling from the Lord in relation to her husband. We will proceed with this study under three basic headings: submitting to your husband, seducing your husband, and surrendering to your husband.

SUBMITTING TO YOUR HUSBAND

Now I know that the mental defenses go up for many women when they hear the dreaded *s*-word, because the concept of submission flies in the face of everything that our culture today teaches, models, and values. But God's Word sits in judgment on our culture, and not vice versa.

One reason that *submission* is such a hated word is that it has been so badly misunderstood and misused, often intentionally, that few people know what it really means. *Submission* is not a bad word, but when people make a good word bad, it becomes bad even though it's good.

I was speaking at a Promise Keepers convention for men at a time when members of the National Association for Women (NOW) were protesting against the idea of submission, saying that it turns women into second-class citizens.

But at the same time that the president of NOW was complaining about the terrible oppression of women being perpetrated by Christians who teach submission, I heard her call the organization's vice president and give her instructions to fulfill a certain task.

We men want and need to hear, "I respect you."

In other words, the president of NOW was asking her subordinate to submit to her leadership. Feminists recognize that submission is appropriate in some roles, and they practice it themselves in these settings. They just don't want to see the concept of submission introduced into marriage because they want to insist that marriage is a totally egalitarian relationship with no one in a leadership position. You see, submission is only a bad idea when it's used in an arena where we don't want it to appear. But it is God's idea, so it can't be bad. In fact, we'll see below that the members of the Godhead practice submission to one another.

The biblical word *submission* means "to line up underneath." It's a voluntary word, an act of the will. In other words, we must choose to submit. Perhaps the best illustration is a yield sign on the highway. Whereas a stop sign means stop, period, no questions asked, you have a choice to make at a yield sign. But your choice carries certain consequences.

If you think you can beat the oncoming car and get out of its way, you may decide to shoot on through the intersection instead of yielding. But if you do, and a collision occurs, you will be at fault because the other vehicle has the right-of-way. Regardless of your view that you were right, the law will consider you to be in rebellion against its statutes.

The same is true in a wife's relationship to her husband. God tells wives to submit to their husbands "as to the Lord" (Ephesians 5:22). A wife may choose to reject that word, but that decision will put her and her marriage on a "collision course" with God's principles.

But the reverse is also true. When we line up in obedience under God's Word, we please Him and open our lives to His blessing. I believe this is the choice you want to make, so let's see what biblical submission that pleases God looks like.

Submitting to Your Husband by Respecting Him

God commands a wife to respect her husband. This word means to hold in high esteem, to lift up. It's closely connected with the word *reverence*. Christian wife, what your husband needs and craves from you more than anything else is respect. While you love to hear, "I love you," we men want and need to hear, "I respect you."

Without respect, men shrivel up and die. I know some women are already objecting that their husbands aren't worthy of respect, and we'll deal with that issue. But I need to make clear that showing respect to your husband is not optional, just as his responsibility to love you with Christlike love is not optional. God can command love and respect on the part of a husband and wife because both are an act of the will, a matter of obedience.

The Bible doesn't give a lot of specifics about how a wife is to show respect to her husband. But we do have one clear example in 1 Peter 3:1–2, where the apostle wrote: "In the same way, you wives, be submissive to your own husbands so that even if any of them are disobedient to the word, they may be won without a word by the behavior of their wives, as they observe your chaste and respectful behavior."

Here are the two concepts of submission and respect side by side again, just as they are in Ephesians 5 (see vv. 22 and 33). Peter reinforced Paul by indicating that the primary way a wife respects her husband is through her submission. But Peter added an important description of what respectful submission looks like.

Peter called it "chaste and respectful behavior," which basically involves a wife's godly attitude that can draw an unbelieving husband to Christ without her having to preach to him, continually criticize his lifestyle, or pin Bible verses to his pillow at night. A wife respects her husband, even if he's an unbeliever, by refusing to browbeat or manipulate him into doing what she wants him to do.

The kind of respect the Bible is talking about here is the kind we all want to be shown at work and among our friends. If your boss constantly stood over you and told you how to do every detail of your job, you'd get very tired of not being shown any respect for having a brain, and you'd probably quit. It takes respect for a wife to forego criticizing or manipulating her husband even when she has a valid point.

Submitting to Your Husband as His Equal

Now at this point some women object that this isn't fair. "Why should I have to submit and defer to my husband when I have a better education than he has and bring home more money than he does?" Or, "If I didn't take charge at home, nothing would get done. I'm much stronger and less passive than my husband."

All of these are issues that may need to be addressed in a marriage, but the biblical doctrine of submission has nothing to do with how much clout a wife brings to the table as opposed to her husband, or who has the stronger personality. To submit is to recognize that God has given the wife the yield sign.

Submission has to do with *function,* not *being.* It does not signify that a wife is inferior to her husband in terms of her worth before God. Peter dealt with that when he told husbands to consider their wives as a "fellow heir of the grace of life" (1 Peter 3:7). Men and women have equal worth in God's eyes.

Submission also doesn't mean that a wife has been relegated to an inferior position of servitude that denies her gifts and abilities and leaves her unfulfilled. How could this be if submission is the will of God?

The woman described in Proverbs 31:10–31 wasn't some passive, mindless person standing around waiting to be told what to do. This lady was awesome. She had her MBA, because the Bible says she negotiated with merchants from afar. She had her real estate license, because she bought and sold property. She also managed the family's finances, supervised a household staff, and had her own ministry to the poor.

But in terms of her marriage, she used her considerable skills in such a way that they enhanced her husband in his role instead of usurping him or tearing him down. Proverbs 31:23 says her husband was one of the leaders in town who was well known, which suggests that he benefited from his wife's ministry.

Submission does not mean that a wife has to deny who she is. But when all of the facts are on the table and a decision has to be made, the wife has the yield sign. She may have equal input to offer, and a wise husband will listen to a wise wife, but he is charged with responsibility for the decision.

Many wives wonder how often this arrangement applies. Let me cite Ephesians 5:24 and then discuss it: "But as the church is subject to Christ, so also the wives ought to be to their own husbands in everything."

The Bible says that wives are to submit to their husbands in every area of life. The example is the church's submission to Christ. In fact, two verses earlier we read, "Wives, be subject to your own husbands, as to the Lord" (v. 22).

This is a sweeping principle, but we need to mention one exception that can arise in a marriage. When a husband requires his wife to do something that is clearly against God's will and would cause her to dishonor her relationship with Christ, then she has a greater duty to obey God and not submit to her husband (see Acts 5:27–29 for a statement of this principle).

Cases like this reinforce the truth that a wife is her husband's equal in terms of her intrinsic worth before God. When God refers to submission, He is talking about the carrying out of a divinely ordained program, which in this case is the home. A home is not designed to function with two heads, just as a human body is not meant to have two heads.

By the way, the greatest example of submission in function on the part of equal beings to accomplish a divine program is not marriage but the Godhead itself. Jesus said, "I and the Father are one" (John 10:30), but throughout His ministry Jesus spoke and acted in submission to His Father (see John 8:29; 12:49). His submission to the Father is also underscored in 1 Corinthians 11:3, which is quoted later.

Christian wife, you are equal to your husband in being made in God's image and being the object of His saving grace. Submission is a voluntary act of obedience to God on your part that does not diminish your worth in any way.

Submitting to Your Husband's Position of Headship

The Bible gives us a very helpful analogy of how submission and authority are to operate in marriage. The relationship between a husband and wife is not that of a master to a slave (although some married folk think it is), but that of a head to a body.

Paul wrote, "I want you to understand that Christ is the head of every man, and the man is the head of a woman, and God is the head of Christ" (1 Corinthians 11:3). The job of the head is to give guidance and direction to the body. The job of the body is to follow the direction of the head.

If your arms or legs start moving independently of signals from your brain, or in rebellion to the signals from your brain, you need to see a doctor because that's a sign of physical sickness.

In the same way, a wife who refuses to follow her husband's leadership is spiritually sick because she is not functioning in line with a body's relationship to its head. Whenever a believer operates outside of God's standard, God does not respond to that person, because He will not participate in or endorse rebellion.

Some Christian women are not getting their prayers answered or seeing God move in their lives as a direct result of their refusal to submit to their husbands. Some husbands are discouraged from taking their rightful leadership roles because they are "sleeping with the enemy." They are married to women who have decided that their job is to find out which way their husbands want to go and head in the opposite direction.

This problem started in the Garden of Eden when the devil persuaded Eve to act as the head and make the decision to disobey God and Adam acted as the body by following Eve in her sin. Now Adam still bore the ultimate responsibility as the head because he abdicated his authority, and the disease of sin was passed through the man. But don't miss the fact that Satan did the great reversal, leading Adam and Eve to switch roles. When that happened, hell broke loose in the family. A woman who wants to be the head of her home invites the devil to take over her family. And the devil has taken over many a family because the wife has refused to submit to the legitimate, biblical authority of her husband. The result is spiritual sickness and dysfunction.

So a wife is to look to her husband for direction the way a body looks to its head. But Satan is going to do everything he can to keep that from happening in your home. He will bring people into your life who will tell you, "Girl, you're crazy to submit to that man. No man is going to tell me what to do!"

You'll also find plenty of reminders that your husband is far from perfect. Now don't misunderstand. This is no excuse for a husband to justify his failure to follow God and to try to be all that God wants him to be. But there's a larger principle at work here, which is this: A husband is his wife's head by *position* even if he is not fulfilling that role in his *practice*. And God calls the wife to recognize and honor that position.

The problem is that we want to respond to a person's practice only instead of that person's position of authority, which we think gives us permission to rebel. So we have wives who refuse to submit to their husbands' leadership because they don't believe the husbands are worthy of their respect.

But a wife owes her husband respect because he is her head by God's design. That's his position—and there are all kinds of situations in life in which we are called to honor and serve leaders who are not fulfilling the ideal.

If employees only worked for bosses who are ideal leaders, there would be massive unemployment in America. Your boss may be a poor leader, but you still do your job and say, "Yes sir, Mr. Jones," or, "Yes sir, Mr. Wilson," because the company says you must acknowledge your leader's position. And the rewards come when you get your paycheck or that promotion.

I know that some Christian wives are facing the trauma and the dilemma that I call trying to follow a parked car. That is, their husbands aren't going anywhere spiritually. God understands this trauma, which is why the Bible adds this crucial qualifier to the command for wives to submit to their husbands: "So that even if any of them [husbands] are disobedient to the word, they may be won without a word by the behavior of their wives" (1 Peter 3:1).

Christian wife, don't ever think that God isn't interested in bringing your unsaved or spiritually weak husband into line. He wants your cooperation in the process, but not in the way many women think their husbands need help. God doesn't need you to be your husband's critic, his conscience, or his mother. Neither does he need you to sit down, fold your arms, and say, "OK, that's it. I'm not going to do what I'm supposed to do until my husband starts doing what he's supposed to do."

So does that mean a wife can't do or say anything to help her husband take his God-ordained role? Of course not. "Without a word" is an idiom that means don't preach at your husband. It doesn't mean you can't communicate your concerns. The idea is to avoid the kind of nagging, condescending, critical conversation that can drive a man further from Christ.

We all know people who are living proof of the fact that years of fussing and cussing and riding someone verbally doesn't produce the desired change. God says it's time for a change of approach.

For a Christian wife, that approach is "chaste and respectful behavior" that a husband can see (1 Peter 3:2). We learned that this is best exemplified by a wife's willing and wholehearted submission to her husband. But we have too many marriages even in the church in which the husband doesn't know what this looks like because he has never seen it.

A wife may object, "Oh no, my husband has seen plenty of submission because I'm always giving in to him." Well, the problem there may be in the word respectful. Some wives take the approach, "Oh yeah, I'll submit to my husband all right, but I'm going to take him down with me and make his life miserable in the process."

There may be a hundred reasons that a husband is not fulfilling his role as the head of the home. But a wife who rebels against her head is only introducing a new element of spiritual sickness and dysfunction into the family.

Earlier we referred to a husband in this situation as a parked car. Admittedly, it's hard to follow a parked car. But there are two ways you can deal with a car in front of you that won't move. You can either get ticked off and start honking your horn and waving your fist at the driver, or you can find out what the problem is and help get the car moving.

I've never seen a car suddenly come to life and take off simply because the person behind it was steaming and yelling and honking. You can practice all of your vocabulary on a stalled car, and it won't get either one of you anywhere.

What a stalled car needs is someone to assist it in moving. That's what God has given to husbands in their wives. God calls a wife to be her husband's helper, to urge and encourage him along in the task of leading his marriage and his home.

But when a wife decides to become a "hurtmate" instead of a helpmate, the marital roles get turned upside down and the Enemy sows spiritual chaos in the home. Even well-meaning wives can do damage by criticizing their husbands and complaining about them. And in the process, the good result they are trying to achieve is actually undermined.

I really believe that there are Christian wives who need to go to their husbands and say something like this: "I am sorry for disrespecting you, and for talking to you disrespectfully in front of the children. I have been unwilling to serve you in the way God expects me to, and I have used your weaknesses as my excuse for not submitting to your leadership."

It's been a long time since some husbands have had a kind word or reassurance from their wives that they're doing something right. You may say, "I'd compliment him if he did something right." Well, he did at least one thing right. He married you!

Women who don't really believe that God can change their husbands through the Holy Spirit's work figure it's now their job, so they are going to help God out. As we move on through 1 Peter 3 we'll see that there is plenty a wife can do to influence her husband. So don't worry that you have to be invisible or mere window dressing in your marriage.

Have you ever seen eagles fly? They are known for soaring and gliding as their wings catch the wind. But did you know that if eagles could not soar, they would crash? Their wings are too heavy for them to flap continually the way some birds do. So eagles flap their wings until they catch an air current, and then they soar.

A lot of wives are trying too hard to make their marriages work, but they can't sustain the weight of what they're doing, and they crash. God says, "I want you to soar on the wind of the Holy Spirit. Position yourself in

Me, and let Me glide your marriage into a changed relationship." When you are doing it God's way, you don't have to flap because you can soar.

SEDUCING YOUR HUSBAND

Some of the fancy department stores on Fifth Avenue in New York City are now using live models in their windows instead of mannequins. I was walking along Fifth Avenue one time when I paused by a store window and saw a live model standing as still as a mannequin, except that she blinked.

Other people must have seen it too, because they were making faces and knocking on the window, trying to get her to mess up. But she held her ground and stood motionless, because there was something more important to her than pleasing the people on the other side of the glass. She was pleasing her employer who was paying her to stand in that window.

Women who want to please the Lord in their marriages often must ignore the people on the other side of the glass. That's because what God is telling them in His Word may go against what many of their friends are telling them and what the television is telling them. But none of us is here to please the onlookers.

The title of this section may cause you to wonder if our focus is on pleasing the Lord or pleasing your husband. But I'm using the concept of seduction in its very basic sense of what is attractive—and in this sense a wife's *inner* attraction is both alluring to her husband and pleasing to God.

We're ready to consider 1 Peter 3:3–4, which addresses the issue of a woman's true beauty. "Your adornment must not be merely external—braiding the hair, and wearing gold jewelry, or putting on dresses; but let it be the hidden person of the heart, with the imperishable quality of a gentle and quiet spirit, which is precious in the sight of God."

Your Inner Adornment

We need to look at the word translated "adornment." This is the Greek word *kosmos,* more familiar to us as cosmos. It is often translated "world" in the New Testament, as when we are told not to love the world (see 1 John 2:15). The basic meaning of cosmos is an "arrangement" or a system. In the case of the world, it refers to a system that leaves God out.

But there's another derivative of this word that we use today, which is *cosmetic.* In this case, as in 1 Peter, the reference is to the way that a woman arranges or organizes herself to make herself attractive to her husband and, by extension, to others around her.

Peter used this word *adornment* for women for two reasons: first, because women are very interested in how they look; and second, because *men* are very interested in how women look.

Women are so oriented toward their appearance that they carry with them the tools they need to keep themselves looking good. Adornment is important to women, so the Bible draws on that reality to call godly wives to adorn or arrange themselves in a certain way, particularly for their husbands.

Just as a woman would make an effort to see that everything is in place with her hair, face, and clothing, so a wife is to adorn herself with that which has deeper value than external beauty. In the context of 1 Peter 3, that adornment includes the submission and respect she shows to her husband—the way she honors and encourages him.

This not only makes a wife attractive to her husband, but it also carries great value with God. Peter described this inner beauty as "a gentle and quiet spirit" (v. 4), which God calls "precious." A woman who wants to please God displays this kind of spirit and regularly checks her "makeup" in the mirror of God's Word to keep herself looking good.

God tells Christian women not to let their attractiveness stop on the outside.

God wants women who know Him to be well arranged and attractive in their spirits. He wants them to be attention-getting in the right way to their husbands and to the world.

Some people think the Bible teaches that to be truly godly, a woman must intentionally neglect her appearance, shun all jewelry or adornment, and wear shabby clothing as evidence that she is holy and not taken up with material things.

That's not what Peter was teaching in 1 Peter 3:3. The translators added the word *merely* to this verse to help us capture the sense of the passage. The Bible does not forbid a woman from caring for or even adorning herself, provided it is modest and in proper taste and the motive is not to draw inappropriate attention to herself. The Bible does not condemn a woman for being attractive, but God tells Christian women not to let their attractiveness stop on the outside.

I believe God wants a wife to be attractive to her husband. That is part of her beauty and charm as a woman. Few women would show contempt for their co-workers and boss by going to work in a disheveled way. A wife needs to show her husband the same respect and honor she gives to her employer.

But as we said earlier, a woman's beauty needs to be tempered by modesty. Paul wrote, "I want women to adorn [the word *kosmos* again] themselves with proper clothing, modestly and discreetly, not with braided hair and gold or pearls or costly garments, but rather by means of good works, as is proper for women making a claim to godliness" (1 Timothy 2:9–10).

This sounds like Paul forbade what Peter permitted. But the idea here is for a woman not to make herself up in a way that draws undue or improper attention to herself. This is important because Paul was writing in the context of worship in the local church. When a woman adorns herself in such a way as to draw people's eyes away from the Lord and onto herself, that's wrong.

In Paul's day, some women wore elaborate hairdos and wove gold and pearls into their hair to attract attention. Clearly, that kind of display is improper for godly women. Modesty is always in order, and that means any piece of clothing that is too low, too high, or too tight is out of bounds.

That needs to be said today as the standards slip further and further away from modesty—and the church is far from exempt. Dressing immodestly suggests that the intent is to lure.

The Content of Your Adornment

A godly woman's true adornment can't be bought at a department store or acquired in the beauty shop. The problem today is that so much of the beauty we see is store-bought. It requires regular trips to the department store, the hair stylist, and the nail salon to maintain. Some women who talk about going to "put on my face" are speaking the truth, because the one they have is not the real person.

Now I don't mean this as criticism, because we've already said there is nothing wrong with being attractive. But when a woman can't distinguish between her real self and her outer adornment, or when she comes to rely on that adornment for her worth and identity, she has gone beyond the biblical standard.

Peter urged women of God not to define themselves by the jewelry or the clothes they wear. The sum total of who you are is much more than that. There's more to the story.

What is the content of a godly woman's adornment? We read about it earlier: "The imperishable quality of a gentle and quiet spirit" (1 Peter 3:4). God's question to women who believe is, Are you trying as hard to be attractive on the inside as you are on the outside? He wants to make sure that your internal beauty is taking precedence over your external beauty. He wants to make sure that He can compliment how you look on the inside.

Peter was speaking in particular about the way a woman appears to her husband. He said that a woman's husband ought to see her inner beauty by the way she conducts herself and responds to him through the willing submission and honor she shows him.

Therefore, a woman who dishonors her husband is showing a poor style, an unattractive internal wardrobe. Your external person, the part that others can see, must be supported by your internal character. That's why Peter called this quality "the hidden person," your spirit at the core of your being, the part of you no one sees.

A Christian wife who may be looking good on the outside, but who cuts her husband with her words, runs him down to her friends and family, and dishonors him in the children's presence is not beautiful by God's definition. If the inner adornment of a woman's spirit is missing or messed up, no amount of jewelry or clothes or any other store-bought beauty enhancement can ultimately hide the ugliness.

Transformed by God's Glory

How does a wife become beautiful on the inside? By allowing herself to be transformed by God's glory. In other words, a woman who wants to please God and become truly alluring to her husband must be a woman who is in passionate pursuit of God, seeking to be in His presence so she can be transformed into the image of His glory.

When God is your focus, Christian wife, He will give you the "imperishable quality" that the Bible calls "a gentle and quiet spirit." This doesn't refer to the quantity of your words but to the quality of your communication. Does that mean a wife won't ever get frustrated or have a bad day or say something she wishes she hadn't said? Of course not. If these were the criteria for godliness, none of us would make it. We all fail, but a woman who exhibits this kind of spirit has a demeanor of kindness. It is said of the woman in Proverbs 31 that "the teaching of kindness is on her tongue" (v. 26).

You say, "Well, I could be like that if I had all the things going for me that this woman had going for her." No, God wants wives who will honor Him whatever their circumstances, and He offers each woman the power to pull this off in the midst of her imperfect setting.

We're talking about a woman's inner beauty, which is something she can't daub on at the last minute the way she might put on makeup before going to a party. By that

I mean that a submissive, gentle spirit has to be woven into a wife's inner being so that kindness is "on her tongue"—the first thing that comes out, in other words.

You see, a person can hide inner ugliness behind a nice smile, nice clothes, and a fresh layer of cosmetics. But what's inside will come out eventually, and God's concern is that what comes out of a godly woman is a spirit that reflects His glory.

A geode is a rock with beautiful crystals inside. These are formed as water that is high in mineral content flows through the rocks. As minerals become trapped in the rock and the water continues to flow, the crystals are formed. And the more the water flows, the more beautiful the crystals become.

Now the external rock begins to wear and weather over time. But inside, the crystal is getting more beautiful as the water continues to flow. That's the picture of a woman in whom and through whom the Spirit of God is flowing. Her external appearance may age, and wrinkles may begin to show, but she grows more beautiful inside with each passing year.

Women who are being transformed by God's glory have nothing to fear from anyone, just as Sarah and other "holy women" of past days "hoped in God" and were submissive to their husbands. A woman who does "what is right" need not be afraid (1 Peter 3:5–6). We'll have a lot more to say about this later.

The Bible uses the word *glory* in another sense that is important for us here. A woman's long hair is said to be a "glory to her" (1 Corinthians 11:15). Women understand this in a way that most men cannot comprehend.

When my wife and I need to go somewhere at seven o'clock, for example, an hour before this she goes before the mirror of her glory. Within an hour she is transformed before my eyes and is looking glorious.

We go to the car, which is inside the garage. That's good, because that way my wife doesn't have to go outside and risk messing up her glory. And when we get into the car, she pulls down the mirror in the visor to check on her glory.

Then, when we arrive at our destination and get on the elevator, there is usually a mirror there too, so she can double-check her glory. And when we get to the place we're going, she runs into some friends and they go off together to the powder room to discuss each other's glory.

A woman wants to feel glorious, and that's fine. But God wants her to work on her inner glory too, so that the outer person is not a covering for an unattractive, harsh, disrespectful spirit.

I can hear a wife saying, "OK, I get the picture. I am supposed to show respect to my husband, and I need to let God's grace flow through me and change me so that I can do what I couldn't do in my own strength.

"But you don't understand. My husband irritates me. He gets on my nerves. He doesn't really deserve my respect or my submission. He doesn't even notice or appreciate the fact that I'm trying to conform myself to God's glory and learn how to let Him work through me."

There are a lot of Christian women who would say amen to that sentiment. Things probably weren't much different in the first century, which is why the last phrase of 1 Peter 3:4 is so important. A woman who seeks to be a woman of God is "precious in [His] sight." This means the "audience" for whom she is doing this is not necessarily her husband. He's just the beneficiary.

The audience is God Himself. As a woman looks to Him, she is transformed. The word *sight* means face-to-face. According to 2 Corinthians 3:18, when we look into the face of God and behold His glory, we are transformed into His image with ever-increasing levels of glory.

In other words, we could say that God becomes a woman's "makeup artist" when she looks to Him for inner transformation. God begins to work on her spirit, and the result is glorious even if the process of applying the makeup isn't always pleasant.

No Hollywood star with her own dressing room, hair stylist, and personal makeup expert has anything on a godly woman who looks to God for her beauty regimen.

God calls a woman like this "precious" to Him. This is the same word used of the perfume that Mary used to anoint Jesus before His death (see John 12:3). This perfume was very costly.

What makes something precious in terms of being very costly? Generally, a precious item is something that is rare. And the rarer it is, the more valuable it is. If the ground were littered with diamonds to be gathered up, they would lose their exceptional value.

A woman who is determined to follow God and allow His glory to shine through her is so precious because she's so rare. Now I didn't say that; God did. The very first thing that's said about the "excellent wife" is the rhetorical question, "Who can find" one like her? (Proverbs 31:10a).

That's another way of saying that such a woman is hard to find. Now let me add that we're speaking of the culture at large. As a pastor, I value the incredible contributions that godly women are making to the body of Christ. It is historically true in America that many churches have been sustained by the presence of faithful, praying women. That's both a tribute to godly women and a call to Christian men to get off the sidelines and get into the game.

But the woman God is talking about is hard to find. And like all rare treasures, "Her worth is far above jewels" (Proverbs 31:10b). A godly wife needs to understand her great value in God's sight, even if her husband doesn't see or appreciate it.

God pays attention to a woman like this, and He works on her behalf. Men may get all worked up about a woman who looks good on the outside, but God's favor is on a woman who fears Him because she is precious in His sight.

When Mary broke her alabaster box and poured the perfume on Jesus, the others thought this was a waste. But to Jesus, her sacrifice was exceedingly precious. He not only defended Mary, but praised her (see Mark 14:9).

God abhors external beauty and adornment that is used as a cloak for pride and rebellion against Him. There is a sobering example of this in Isaiah 3, where the Lord has a word of rebuke and judgment for the women of Judah. It's worth quoting this passage in depth:

> The Lord said, "Because the daughters of Zion are proud and walk with heads held high and seductive eyes, and go along with mincing steps and tinkle the bangles on their feet, therefore the Lord will afflict the scalp of the daughters of Zion with scabs, and the Lord will make their foreheads bare." In that day the Lord will take away the beauty of their anklets, headbands, crescent ornaments, dangling earrings, bracelets, veils, headdresses, ankle chains, sashes, perfume bottles, amulets, finger rings, nose rings, festal robes, outer tunics, cloaks, money purses, hand mirrors, undergarments, turbans and veils. Now it will come about that instead of sweet perfume there will be putrefaction; instead of a belt, a rope; instead of well-set hair, a plucked-out scalp, instead of fine clothes, a donning of sackcloth; and branding instead of beauty. (vv. 16–24)

God said He was going to make these women's outsides look like their insides because they didn't spend their time looking good on the inside for Him. They were only interested in their appearance and the attention they could bring their way. But God said He would make their beauty perish.

However, a woman who is being transformed by God's glory has an inner beauty that is imperishable.

The Way to Change Your Husband

There would probably be a lot of wives getting in line if someone was offering advice on how to change their husbands. Well, Peter gave us Holy Spirit–inspired advice on the best way a wife can influence and change her husband. The only reason it isn't tried and proven more is that it isn't the advice many wives want to hear.

That's because the focus in 1 Peter 3 is on a wife's calling to become a woman who pleases God and through whom He can work to bring her husband into line. Now that doesn't mean the husbands get off easy, because God has some pointed challenges for them too. But the emphasis here is on a wife's character.

Remember the advice we often heard when we were single people looking for mates? We were often told that it's more important to *be* the right person than to find the right person.

That was sound advice when we were single, and it's still sound advice today. One reason is that it is very hard to change another person. So if you go into marriage thinking you are going to whip your spouse into shape, you are setting yourself up for years of frustration.

I can hear some long-suffering wife saying, "Amen. I've been trying to change my husband for years, and nothing has worked." That's why God says, "If you will allow Me to work on you, I will take care of your husband too."

It's true that a woman who exhibits a godly, gentle spirit is precious in God's sight. But He will also make her precious in her husband's sight. When God goes to work on a wife's inner spirit with His divine makeup kit, He can make her so mesmerizing and so attractive to her husband that he doesn't think about her the way he used to think and he doesn't see her the way he used to see her.

This is not a blanket guarantee that every husband of every godly wife will either get saved or get his Christian life on track and start taking the spiritual leadership in his home. It may take years, or in some cases the husband may never get the picture. But wives' godly behavior is still of incredible value to God.

Nothing is automatic, but the formula we're reading about in 1 Peter 3—a wife's inner transformation by God—is one of the most effective change formulas for marriages I have ever seen. And the charm of this kind of beauty is that it doesn't fade or wrinkle with time like physical beauty, and so its fading glory doesn't have to be hidden behind lotions and creams and layers of cosmetics. In fact, true inner beauty gets more attractive with the passing years.

Christian wife, your external beauty probably played a role in winning your husband, because men respond to what they see. But it's your internal beauty that will change him. You say, "But my husband can't see internal beauty."

He doesn't have to. Your spiritual adornment is precious to God, and when God sees it He will do what you can't do and work where you can't reach. He will go to work on your husband.

Now in case you're feeling put upon as the one who has to do all the conforming to Christ's glory, let me give you a model and an example to follow that I hope will encourage you.

For this we need to go back to the very opening phrase of 1 Peter 3, where we read, "In the same way, you wives be submissive . . ." I've saved that for now because this is rich. This phrase makes us ask, "In the same way as what?" Well, in this case the reference is to the example of Jesus Christ:

> For you have been called for this purpose, since Christ also suffered for you, leaving you an example for you to follow in His steps, who committed no sin, nor was any deceit found in His mouth; and while being reviled, He did not revile in return; while suffering, He uttered no threats, but kept entrusting Himself to Him who judges righteously; and He Himself bore our sins in His body on the cross. (1 Peter 2:21–24a)

Just as Jesus had to trust God in a bad situation, so many wives must trust God in a bad situation. Jesus did not pay His accusers back with degrading and belittling words. He committed Himself to God and pursued His will even though it meant the cross.

Did Jesus' godly reaction to suffering produce change in others? It produced the greatest change in human history! Jesus had no faults or sins of His own to worry about. But even as the sinless Son of God, Jesus' response to His suffering was to bear it patiently and allow God to do His complete work.

A woman whose desire is to please God can respond to her circumstances "in the same way," no matter what the challenge.

SURRENDERING TO YOUR HUSBAND

Jesus' example also helps us see what it means to surrender to God's divine plan. Christ willingly lay down on the cross and stretched out His arms to be nailed because it was the will of His Father.

There are, no doubt, many wives who would say they feel almost as though they're being crucified by their marriages. From their perspective, it seems as if they are being asked to lie down, stretch out their arms, and surrender themselves to their husbands, who may or may not appreciate their sacrifice and treat them accordingly. And they fear that act of surrender.

Since no husband and no marriage is perfect, the issue of surrender is a difficult one for many wives. That's because, as we have seen, God calls a wife to respect and submit to her husband even when he may not be worthy of her respect or when there is a difference of opinion and the wife has a valid point. She must honor her husband's position as head of the home in order to accomplish a common program.

And when a wife does this out of respect for her husband and obedience to God, He responds to her obedience and liberates her from her fears. That's the point I want us to see in 1 Peter 3:5–6, the final two verses in this passage that is devoted to wives.

We would all like to be liberated. But there are too many women, even in the family of God, who are prisoners of their own rebellion and stubbornness because they refuse to recognize or yield to the divine order for marriage.

Instead of doing things God's way and trusting Him for the results, these women are using their tongues to dishonor and put down their husbands in the hope that they can break free from what they perceive as the bondage of marriage. But instead of freedom, they find themselves still incarcerated in a bad situation, because God will never honor rebellion.

Adam needed help, for sure. He didn't have it all together by himself.

The Bible says that a wife who honors God creates an opportunity to win her husband over without lecturing, badgering, or demeaning him. However, that a husband will eventually come around is a general principle and not an ironclad guarantee for everyone. The possibility is hard for some wives to believe, because they don't see any way their husbands will ever come around without their intervention. But this is what God says, so the question for Christian wives is whether they are going to let God be true even if everyone else is found to be a liar (see Romans 3:4).

There should be plenty of wives ready to give God's way a try, because they've been trying it their way for years and it hasn't worked yet. Lasting spiritual change is the work of God the Holy Spirit, not the product of our efforts.

Peter went back into biblical history to point out some women who understood this principle and put it to work in their lives. "For in this way in former times the holy women also, who hoped in God, used to adorn themselves, being submissive to their own husbands" (1 Peter 3:5).

Models of Godly Surrender

Part of the problem we're dealing with today in marriage is the lack of godly examples of husbands and wives who are doing marriage by the Book and seeing God honor their relationship. In this no-absolutes, no-rules generation, it's getting harder and harder to find real-life examples of what God designed marriage to be. In one sense this shouldn't surprise us, because we've already seen that a holy woman is rare, like a precious jewel. And I might add holy *men* are getting harder and harder to find too. Now in the context of 1 Peter 3, a holy woman is someone who trusts in God and is submissive to her husband, truly honoring and respecting him.

Let's make sure we understand what's being said

here. A woman who disrespects her husband and dishonors his position cannot be considered a holy woman in God's sight. "Holy" means set apart for God, which is an internal, invisible spiritual commitment that is made in the heart.

But the Bible also says that we can tell what is in people's hearts by their words and actions. And so it is here. These women of old who trusted God and were set apart for Him demonstrated their faith by the way they honored their husbands.

The point is inescapable. Christian wife, don't tell me you are close to God while you are in rebellion against your husband's leadership, putting him down and battling him for control. The Bible says the holy women of old didn't do that. They reverenced their husbands, even if they didn't always agree with them.

In some cases, mothers are setting their daughters up to dishonor their future husbands. How many times have you heard a mother say, "My daughter had better find a strong man or she will run right over him"?

What that does is program the daughter to look for the weaknesses in a man that she can use as an excuse to take over and rule the relationship—or at least to fight for her way if she does marry a strong man.

We've got this marriage thing all messed up. God said of Adam's need for a mate, "I will make him a helper suitable for him" (Genesis 2:18). Now Adam needed help, for sure. He didn't have it all together by himself. He needed a helper, but our generation has largely misunderstood what this word means.

What It Means to Help

Let's start with the men on this one. When some men hear the word *helper,* they think of someone who is going to cook, clean, do the laundry, and keep the kids quiet while the man watches his ball game.

Television sitcoms are full of these marriage portrayals, and the programs usually get a lot of laughs. But there's nothing funny about a husband who interprets *helper* simply as a maid, cook, and baby-sitter. A woman doesn't have to be a wife to fulfill any of these roles. You can hire people to do these tasks.

Now don't misunderstand. This doesn't mean a wife can neglect or pass off her obligations at home. There is no substitute for her touch in the home, but if that's all her role consists of, then something is wrong because this is not the primary way that a wife serves as a helper to her husband.

The primary way that a wife helps her husband is to help him become the leader that God has appointed him to be. A wife ought to be her husband's chief fan, chief encourager, and chief support system. But she can't help her husband take the lead if she is constantly tearing him down or fighting him for control.

In the Bible, a helper is someone who comes alongside another person to lift and build up that person. Jesus called the Holy Spirit our "Helper" in John 14:16. The Spirit's role is a good example of the way a helper works. Jesus said that the Spirit would not magnify Himself, but would glorify Jesus (John 16:13–14).

Now a wife may be saying, "If that's what being a helper means, I don't want to do it. Why should I spend my time glorifying my husband and lifting him up? The only way I can do that is by denying myself and my gifts and becoming my husband's doormat. If he gets all the glory, that means I don't get any. Besides, I've got more education and a better job than he has."

That assessment may seem harsh, but it's exactly how some wives view the idea of being their husbands' helpers. Is it an accurate assessment? Not at all, and the Holy Spirit's position in the Godhead proves it.

The Spirit is very God of very God, coequal in essence with the Father and the Son. He lost nothing of His deity when He became the Helper and took the role of glorifying Christ. This was a voluntary submission among spiritual equals, just as Christ's submission to the Father during His earthly ministry was a voluntary submission to accomplish the plan of redemption.

A wife who is committed to obey God and live as a holy woman before Him does not have to surrender her person to honor and submit to her husband. In fact, any husband with any sense is going to turn around and honor and lift up his wife when he is empowered by her to take the role God called him to fulfill.

If being a helper honors God and builds up their marriages, why aren't more wives doing this? Because they aren't hanging out with the holy women. Instead, they're getting their input from their unholy girlfriends, watching unholy television, listening to unholy radio, and reading unholy books. Peter said that a woman who wants to get this marriage thing right needs to be spending time in the right company.

Where is a Christian wife, particularly a young woman who is new in her marriage, going to find holy women like this? The Bible says she ought to be finding them in the church:

> Older women likewise are to be reverent in their behavior, not malicious gossips nor enslaved to much wine, teaching what is good, so that they may encourage the young women to love their husbands, to love their children, to be sensible, pure, workers at home, kind, being subject to their own husbands, so that the word of God will not be dishonored. (Titus 2:3–5)

The older women in view here are not only those further along in age, but women who are spiritually mature and able to offer a godly example. You don't go to a person who has been married for five months, or married five times, for advice on how to respect and submit to your husband.

What a lot of Christian wives need are godly women who won't be telling them, "Girl, I'd leave him if I were you," or, "I wouldn't take that," when times get tough.

Of course, we're not talking about a wife enduring beatings and abuse from a husband who is out of control because she thinks that's what God wants her to do. There is no excuse for abuse. But a wife who wants to fulfill her biblical calling and be a helper to her husband needs holy women who are going to give her holy information on what it means to be a holy wife.

Titus 2:5 gives us the ultimate motivation for wives to help build godly marriages. God isn't concerned about a woman pleasing her society friends or her feminist co-workers. His concern is the honor of His Word and the glory of His name. When marriages are out of sync with God's will, disaster is waiting to happen and God's holy name is at risk of being dishonored.

Satan's Great Reversal

We can see this disaster unfold in the first marriage in history. In his temptation of Eve in the Garden of Eden, Satan induced her to disregard and ignore Adam and assume the role of headship Adam was supposed to play (see Genesis 3:1–6).

Adam was at fault for his lack of leadership, and the Bible lays the ultimate responsibility for the entrance of sin at his feet. Every man will be held accountable for what happens in his home. God will not ask a husband about his wife, but about what he did with the responsibility of leadership that he was given. But Eve's actions in Eden still played a critical role in helping create this disaster.

The reason I say that Eve ignored Adam in yielding to Satan's temptation is that according to Genesis 3:6, Adam was with her when this happened. We tend to think of Adam as being absent, but the Bible says she gave the fruit "to her husband with her."

At this moment Adam was being a passive non-leader,

apparently failing to fulfill his role as the serpent tempted Eve. But instead of handing the leadership off to Adam and forcing him to take the lead, Eve took the lead and reversed the couple's roles. When that happened, Satan had them.

The result, of course, was a curse on every aspect of creation, including the marriage relationship. God told Eve, "Your desire will be for your husband, and he will rule over you" (Genesis 3:16).

Some people take this to refer to a woman's sexual desire, but that's not what this means. The woman's desire would be to rule the man, and he would also desire to rule because he was made to rule. The result is what we call the battle of the sexes, with the woman rebelling against the man's attempts to rule over her.

That battle is still going on today as a product of the curse. But when we come to Christ, we are redeemed from the curse. Satan doesn't want wives to know that they don't have to fight anymore for that position of headship. He doesn't want wives to discover that if they will honor God by respecting and submitting to their husbands, they can stop struggling to fill a position they were never designed to fill and begin enjoying peace in their hearts, even if their husbands don't respond properly to their submission.

A Wife's Trust in God

But we need to say again that this doesn't just happen. The key to pulling this off, the motivation that led the holy women of old to reverence their husbands, is that they "hoped in God" (1 Peter 3:5). God wants to know if a woman trusts Him and really believes His Word.

Focusing your trust on the Lord means that you recognize there is something bigger going on here than your respect for your husband. The Bible tells wives to submit to their husbands "as to the Lord" (Ephesians 5:22).

You see, God overrules your husband in terms of authority. Here is the answer to those who think the biblical framework makes a man the absolute ruler in his kingdom with his wife and children as his indentured servants. This is why a wife must go against her husband when he tries to make her do something that is contrary to God's clearly revealed will.

Now that is the exception, because Ephesians 5 goes on to say that a wife is to be subject to her husband "in everything" (v. 24). How can a wife do that? By putting her faith in the Lord and aligning herself with His established order.

I know at this point you might be saying, "Tony, I'm afraid to do that because I'm afraid my husband will take advantage of my submissive spirit." I hear what you are saying, and we're going to address that fear in a minute because God also hears what you are saying.

A wife's trust is to be in the Lord. It's one thing to trust when things are fine and a husband is fulfilling his roles as leader and lover. But it's another story altogether to trust God when the husband isn't doing his part. That's why a woman's eyes need to be on the Lord, not on her husband. Her perspective can make all the difference. With her faith in God, a wife can see things that others can't see.

I was reminded of this by the story of the teenager who lost a contact lens while playing basketball with his buddies in the driveway. He looked all over the driveway for the lens, but couldn't find it. So with great reluctance he went inside and told his mother what had happened. His mother went outside and found the lens in about two minutes.

Her son was amazed. "Mom, how did you do that so fast?"

"Oh," she said, "that's easy. We weren't looking for the same thing."

"What do you mean?"

"Well, Son, you were looking for a piece of plastic. I was looking for a hundred and fifty dollars."

That mother and son had radically different perspectives. You may look at your husband, or look around you at other people, and say, "Submission doesn't make sense." But when you see things through the eyes of faith, life becomes clearer. You may not see in your husband what you want to see, but you'll never be disappointed if your eyes are on Christ.

A Wife's Surrender to God

There's no question that a woman surrenders some things when she gets married. She surrenders her family name, the financial and personal independence she had when she was single, and even her destiny to a large degree because her future is now inextricably tied to her husband's.

That's a problem to some women, because when their marriage doesn't turn out to be all that they thought it would be, they spend all of their time trying to get back everything they surrendered. And that means a battle.

As I deal with marriages like this, I often discover at least part of the problem is that the wife has never really given her husband honor—and I mean as a daily pattern, not as a once-in-a-while tip of the cap to his position.

Before you go to war to get back what you surrendered, consider what can happen when you make it a priority to honor your husband and willingly submit to him even when he is in the wrong. What can happen is that when you are lined up properly under God, you get yourself out of the way so God can deal with your husband.

But if you don't believe that God can reach your husband, you're going to keep putting yourself between your husband and God and block God's movement in his life. When you surrender, God takes over and fights the battle for you.

We find a classic illustration of this principle in the Old Testament story of Nabal, Abigail, and David in 1 Samuel 25. Nabal was a rich farmer whose men and livestock were guarded by David's men while David was on the run from Saul. But when David sent men to Nabal to seek supplies in appreciation of the men's defense of Nabal's property, Nabal treated them badly and insulted David, sending them away empty-handed and hungry.

David was ticked off and planned to kill Nabal for the insult and his refusal to give them what they needed. But Nabal, whose very name meant "fool," had a very wise wife named Abigail. As soon as she heard about the terrible thing her foolish husband had done, she took David a large supply of good things from the farm and pleaded with him not to carry out his plan and put a stain on his future kingship.

David blessed God when he realized that Abigail had kept him from taking revenge on Nabal. Abigail saved Nabal's life, but the news of how close he came to dying caused Nabal's fool heart to go into cardiac arrest. He died ten days later, and the Bible says that God struck him (v. 38).

The point is that Abigail did the right thing by pleading for Nabal's life even when he didn't deserve her intercession. Instead of adding to the problem, Abigail cleared the way for God to deal with her husband. And the end of the story is that Abigail went from being the wife of a fool to the wife of a king when David married her.

Peter had an example of godly surrender in mind when he wrote his first letter: "Just as Sarah obeyed Abraham, calling him lord" (1 Peter 3:6a). Let's stop there.

When this passage is read people usually get hung up on the term *lord,* which makes it sound like Abraham was some Middle Eastern sheik who expected everyone around him to bow and scrape. You may see that kind of thing on the old late-night movies, but that's not the case here.

This was a term of respect that Sarah used to honor Abraham. In other words, her respect was verbal as well as visual. She honored her husband in both word and action.

When you turn on the television, you don't want a picture without sound, or vice versa. Both sight and sound are needed to get the most out of a television. A wife's honor for her husband needs to be the same way.

Now if you know the story of Abraham and Sarah, you'll recall that Abraham didn't always deserve Sarah's respect. On two occasions, in Genesis 12 and 20, Abraham wimped out and lied to foreign kings about his relationship with Sarah when he thought his neck was on the line. Abraham's actions jeopardized Sarah's purity in each case. God shut down two kingdoms to protect Sarah, and she still spoke to and treated Abraham with respect.

When God has a woman to work with who is willing to surrender to Him, He will move mountains and disrupt kingdoms when necessary to act in her behalf. But the biggest example of this in Sarah's life is not the two times I mentioned above, but the miraculous birth of Isaac.

Isaac's birth was a miracle because Sarah was ninety years old and Abraham was one hundred. God first told Abraham that he and Sarah were going to have a child, and Abraham laughed (see Genesis 17:15–17).

Then God came back later and told Abraham again that Sarah was going to have a son. This time, Sarah overheard the promise and laughed (Genesis 18:10–12). She laughed because Abe was even older than she was and was in no condition to father a child. Sarah laughed because from a human standpoint having a child with Abraham was impossible.

In other words, Sarah wasn't laughing because she refused to believe that God could do the impossible. The Lord responded to her laughter by saying to Abraham, "Is anything too difficult for the Lord?" (Genesis 18:14).

That settled the issue for Abraham and Sarah. How do I know that? Because the author of Hebrews wrote, "By faith even Sarah herself received ability to conceive, even beyond the proper time of life, since she considered Him faithful who had promised" (Hebrews 11:11).

What this tells us is that after a moment of understandable doubt, Sarah surrendered to the Lord and to Abraham that day in her tent when she heard God's promise of the impossible. If you're a wife who is dealing with a seemingly impossible husband and an impossible marriage, maybe it's time for you to say to God, "Lord, even if this thing doesn't change, I'm going to stop doubting and start trusting You."

The Freedom of Surrender

Now we're ready for what may be the best part of this whole issue of a wife's submission to and reverence for her husband. There is freedom from fear awaiting the woman who is willing to cast herself and her marriage upon the Lord.

For most of us, surrender and freedom don't go together. After all, what happens when a fugitive or a soldier surrenders? He loses his freedom and goes either to jail or to a prisoner-of-war camp.

God has a word of assurance for a wife who is willing to do things His way.

But the reverse is true for a woman whose desire is to be a godly wife. When she makes the determination to surrender to God's plan by honoring and respecting her husband, she discovers true freedom. The second half of 1 Peter 3:6 says this: "You have become her [Sarah's] children if you do what is right without being frightened by any fear."

What fear is this referring to? We alluded to it above. It's the fear of a wife who says, "I'm afraid to submit to my husband because I'm afraid he will take advantage of me and use my submission to lord it over me. So I'm going to hold on to part of the control so he won't run roughshod over me."

This kind of reaction is very natural. It's scary for any of us to think about giving up control and surrendering our rights and our preferences to another person.

But we're not talking about having a natural marriage here. We're talking about a *super*natural marriage. Anyone can have a natural marriage, meaning one in which the husband and wife are in conflict and there is a constant battle for control involving "my rights and what I want."

But God has a word of assurance for a wife who is willing to do things His way. "You have nothing to be afraid of, because I see your heart and I know where you are. You are in My sight and in My care. I can deal with your husband if you will align yourself with My will."

Remember Sarah. She was tucked away in a tent in the middle of nowhere in a desolate land to which she had come with Abraham. She was married to a man who had his moments of weakness even though he was a great man of faith.

What's more, Sarah was far too old to have any hope of having a child, and Abraham was even older and less capable of fathering a child. But Sarah believed God could bring a baby out of two dead bodies. God saw Sarah's heart, He knew where she was, and she got her miracle.

You may say, "You've got that right. It would take a miracle for my husband to become the spiritual leader and understanding lover the Bible talks about. I want to see that happen, but I'm afraid to surrender."

God's answer is, "Do not be afraid. I see your heart, and I know where you are. Trust Me."

If your desire is to obey God by honoring your husband, you don't need to fear anyone or any situation. Don't let any fear keep you from experiencing God's best in your marriage. Then, like Sarah, watch God give you your miracle.

THE URBAN ALTERNATIVE

The Philosophy

Dr. Tony Evans and TUA believe the answer to transforming our culture comes from the inside out and from the bottom up. We believe the core cause of the problems we face is a spiritual one; therefore, the only way to address them is spiritually. And that means the proclamation and application of biblical principles to the four areas of life—the individual, the family, the church, and the community. We've tried a political, social, economic, and even a religious agenda. It's time for a kingdom agenda.

The Purpose

We believe that when each biblical sphere of life functions properly, the net result is evangelism, discipleship, and community impact. As people learn how to govern themselves under God, they then transform the institutions of family, church, and government from a biblically based kingdom perspective.

The Programs

To achieve our goal we use a variety of strategies, methods, and resources for reaching and equipping as many people as possible.

- Broadcast Media
  The Urban Alternative reaches hundreds of thousands of people each day with a kingdom-based approach to life through its daily radio program, weekly television broadcast, and the Internet.

- Leadership Training
  Our national Church Development Conference, held annually, equips pastors and lay leaders to become agents of change. Teaching biblical methods of church ministry has helped congregations renew their sense of mission and expand their ministry impact.

- Crusades/Conferences
  Crusades are designed to bring churches together across racial, cultural, and denominational lines to win the lost. TUA also seeks to keep these churches together for ongoing fellowship and community impact. Conferences give Christians practical biblical insight on how to live victoriously in accordance with God's Word and His kingdom agenda in the four areas of life—personal, family, church, and community.

- Resource Development
  We are fostering lifelong learning partnerships with the people we serve by providing a variety of published materials. We offer books, audiotapes,

videos, and booklets to strengthen people in their walk with God and ministry to others.

- Project Turn-Around
  PTA is a comprehensive church-based community impact strategy. It addresses such areas as economic development, education, housing, health revitalization, family renewal and reconciliation. To model the success of the project, TUA invests in its own program locally. We also assist other churches in tailoring the model to meet the specific needs of their communities, while simultaneously addressing the spiritual and moral frame of reference.

* * *

For more information, a catalog of Dr. Tony Evans's ministry resources, and a complimentary copy of Dr. Evans's monthly devotional magazine,
call (800) 800-3222 or
write TUA at P.O. Box 4000, Dallas TX 75208.
or log on to TonyEvans.org.

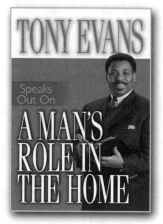
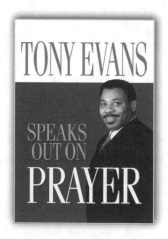

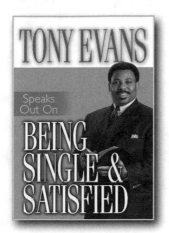

Being Single and Satisfied

Tony Evans takes a brief but insightful look at what the Bible teaches us about being single and finding contentment in that calling. He shares that, finding satisfaction requires that singles maintain moral purity, wait with the right mentality while understanding your mortality.

ISBN: 978-0-8024-4371-7

Other books in the *Tony Evans Speaks Out Series*

Sexual Purity   978-0-8024-4387-8

Single Parenting   978-0-8024-4388-5

Divorce & Remarriage   978-0-8024-4386-1

Gambling & the Lottery   978-0-8024-4385-4

Spiritual Warfare   978-0-8024-4369-4

Fasting   978-0-8024-4366-3

Heaven & Hell   978-0-8024-4367-0